This book is dedicated to dog lovers everywhere.
-Hayley Rose

This is the
story of **Oodle** the Poodle
and how she had six cute little
SCHNOODLES.

It all happened one day,
a long time ago,
at a place they call
THE **Ruffington**
DOG SHOW.

Oodle, you see, was a
prize-winning pup
with eight BLUE ribbons
and eight GOLD cups.

But this show was DIFFERENT, Oodle thought.
This show had something
the others had not...

Bauzer the Schnauzer

Bauzer
the Schnauzer was HANDSOME and TOUGH.
When **Bauzer** walked by,
all the girls would shout out,
"RUFF RUFF."

Then knock-knock-knock—
 came a knock at the door.
"Oodle," said the voice, "it's ten minutes to four."

"All dogs take your places—all in a row."
Then, one by one, they all started to show.

The arena was PACKED as they all pranced around.
A POODLE, a SCHNAUZER, a PUG, and a HOUND.

They took center stage with **style** and **grace**.
The fans went W!LD.
Cheers filled up the place.

With a JUMP and a twirl all perfectly done, she couldn't be beat. Oodle thought she had won.

But then came a SHUDDER, a GASP, and a SHOUT.
"What's that on the floor? Oh, no, Oodle, WATCH OUT!"

She let out a cry, "I'm STUCK! IT'S TOO LATE!"

Would this pink bubble gum now decide Oodle's fate?
"How could this be? It's so sticky—so sweet."
This PINK bit of goodness now stuck to her feet.

Bauzer turned and thought, "I should do the right thing."
Then, his heart skipped a beat;
it *FLUTTERED*; it *ZINGED*.

"I had to help free you," Bauzer said with a smile.

He had a CRUSH too, all the same, all the while.

Their chances of WINNING now not very good,
but they didn't mind;
they both understood.

So CONGRATULATIONS went out to the pug,
who won first place, a ribbon, a hug.

Now, don't be sad. You see, Oodle won too.
Oodle won Bauzer
and a date at the zoo.

Poodle Fun Facts:

Poodles are allergy-friendly! Their unique coat doesn't shed.

Poodles come in three sizes: Standard, Miniature, and Toy.

Schnauzer Fun Facts:

Schnauzers have excellent hearing, and they can hear frequencies twice as high as humans.

Unlike the rest of the terrier group, schnauzers come from Germany, instead of the British Isles.

Pug Fun Facts:

A group of pugs is called a grumble.

A pug's tail generally has some sort of curl or twist to it, but the "double curl" is most desirable.

Hound Fun Facts:

Hounds fall into two main groups which are classified as either scent hounds or sighthounds.

Hounds vary greatly from the small and long dachshund to the tall and lean greyhound or the massive Irish wolfhound.

basset hound

To schedule an appearance or to gush about how much we love dogs, please visit: www.HayleyRose.com

Published in 2023 by Flowered Press
Copyright 2019 by Hayley Rose

Text by Hayley Rose
Illustrations by Gabby

ISBN: 978-1-950842-28-5 (hardcover)
978-1-950842-35-3 (paperback)

Library of Congress Control Number:
2022913650

All Rights Reserved. No part of this publication may be reproduced, stored in a retrieval system or transmitted by any form or by any means, electronic, recording or otherwise without the prior permission in writing from the publisher.

Flowered Press
8776 E. Shea Blvd, #106-213
Scottsdale, AZ 85260

Printed in China

Hayley Rose

is a chocolate-loving writer and goat yoga enthusiast. As the author of several successful children's books and an award-winning line of gratitude coloring journals, Hayley hopes to inspire a love of reading through educational and humorous stories. Hayley lives in Arizona with her mini schnauzer, Blanche.

www.HayleyRose.com

Gabby Corriea

is a self-taught digital artist who can't go a day without chocolate, peanut butter and coffee. For the past ten years, she has been illustrating for authors, bringing their stories to life. From graphic novels to picture books to caricature portraits, Gabby loves the imagination and creativity that goes into story-telling with images. In her free time, she enjoys the outdoors and lives with her boyfriend and two Jack Russel terriers in Cape Town, South Africa.

www.GabbyCorreia.com